I0442284

DOLPHIN
COLORING BOOK
FOR ADULTS

AN ADULT COLORING BOOK OF DOLPHINS FEATURING 40 DOLPHIN DESIGNS IN A VARIETY OF PATTERNS

ADULT COLORING WORLD

ISBN-13: 978-1522918127

ISBN-10: 1522918124

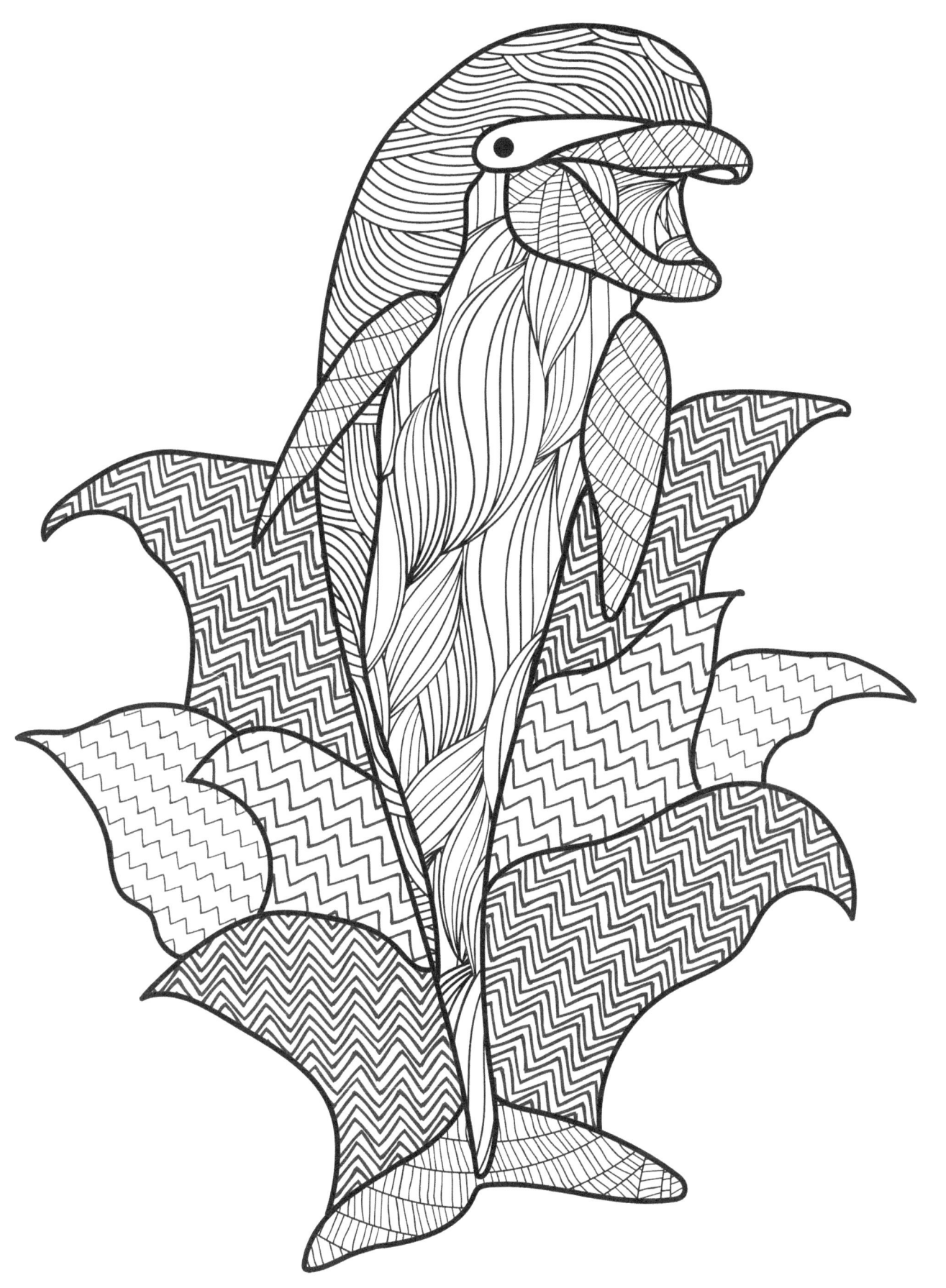

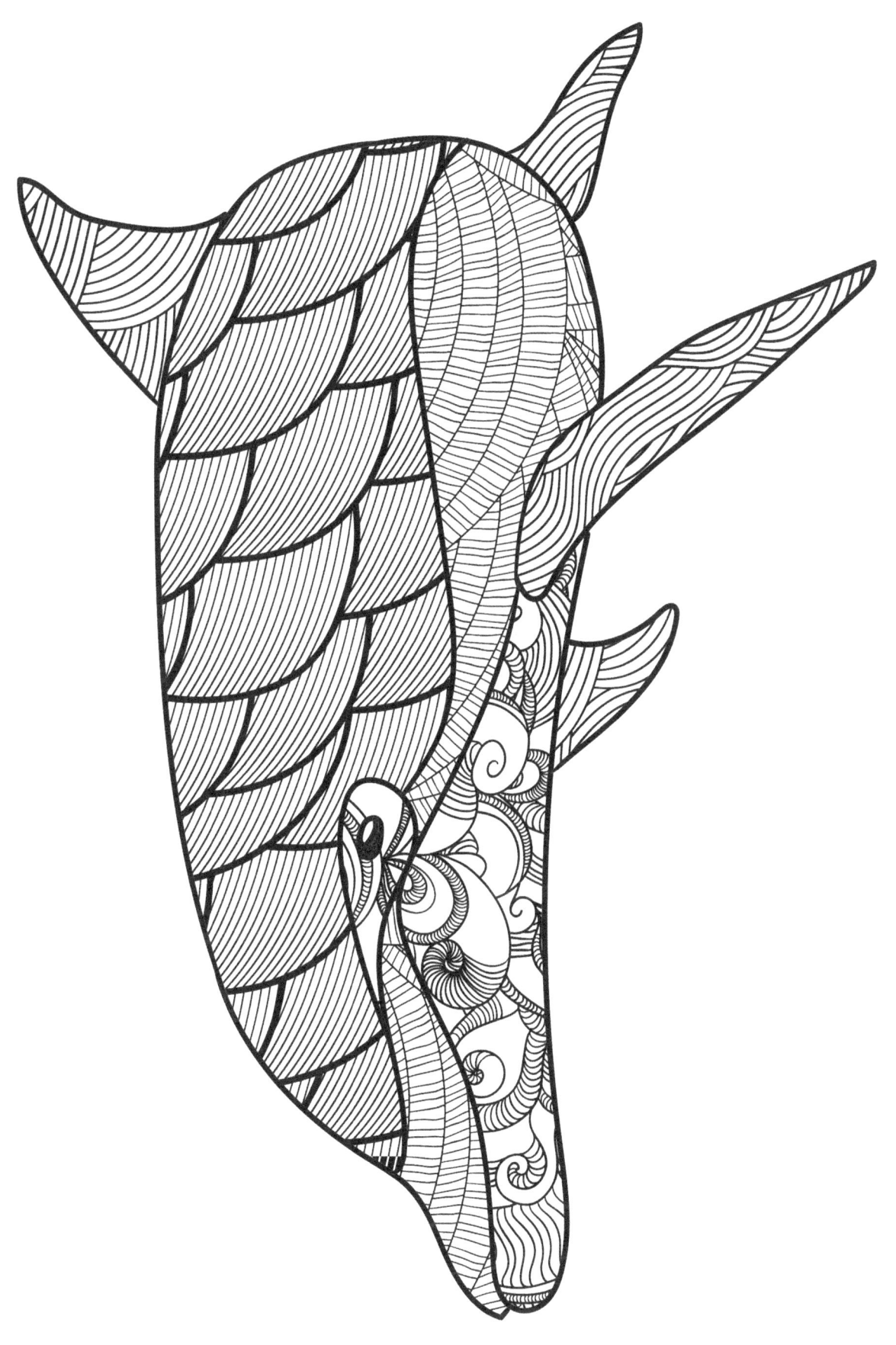

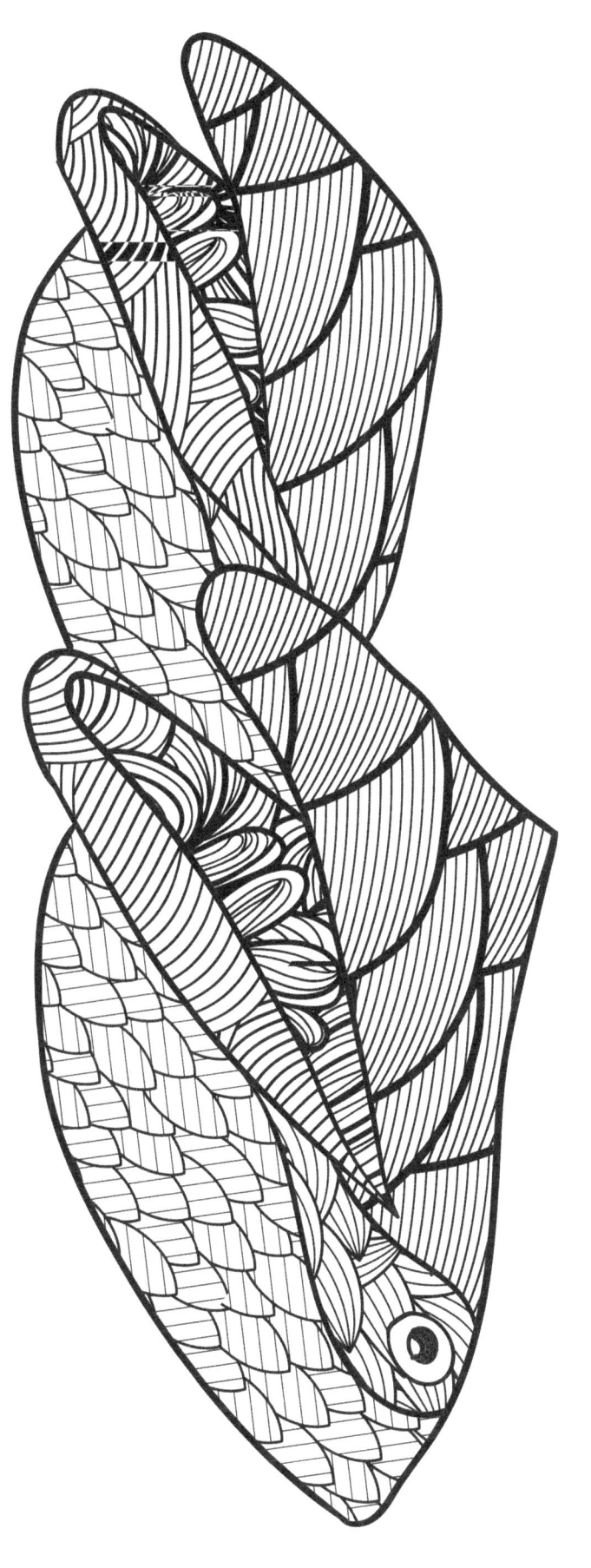

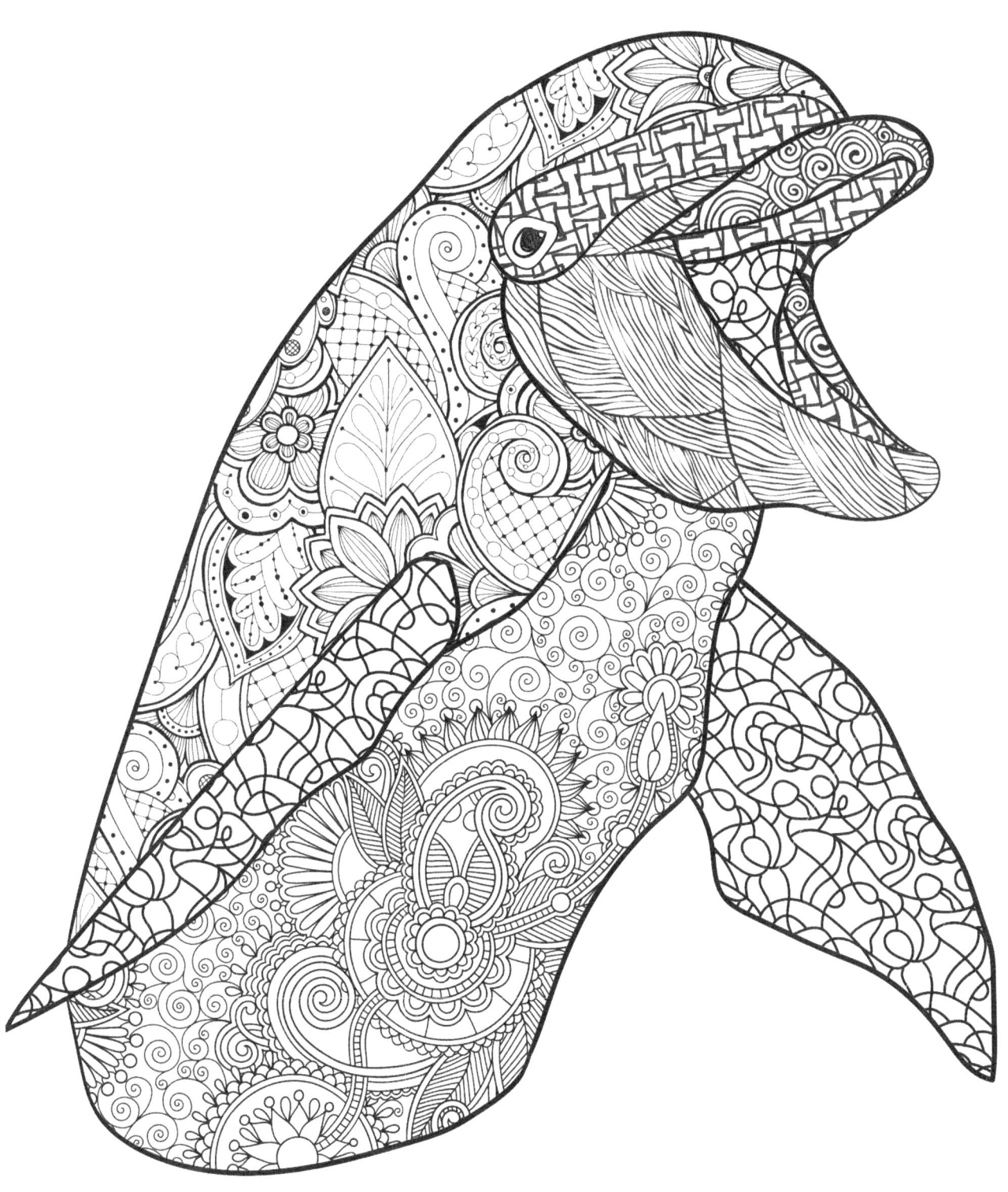

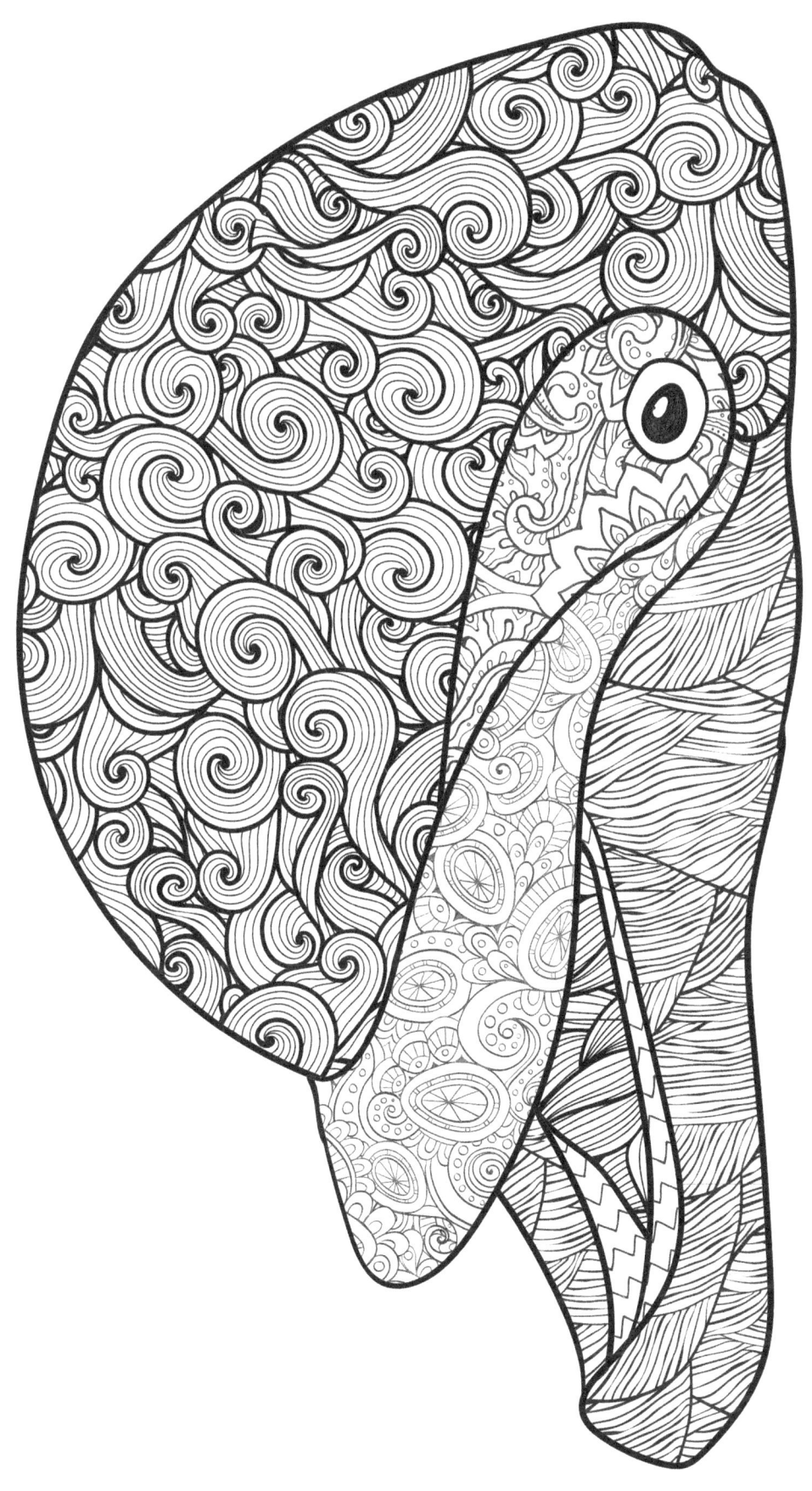

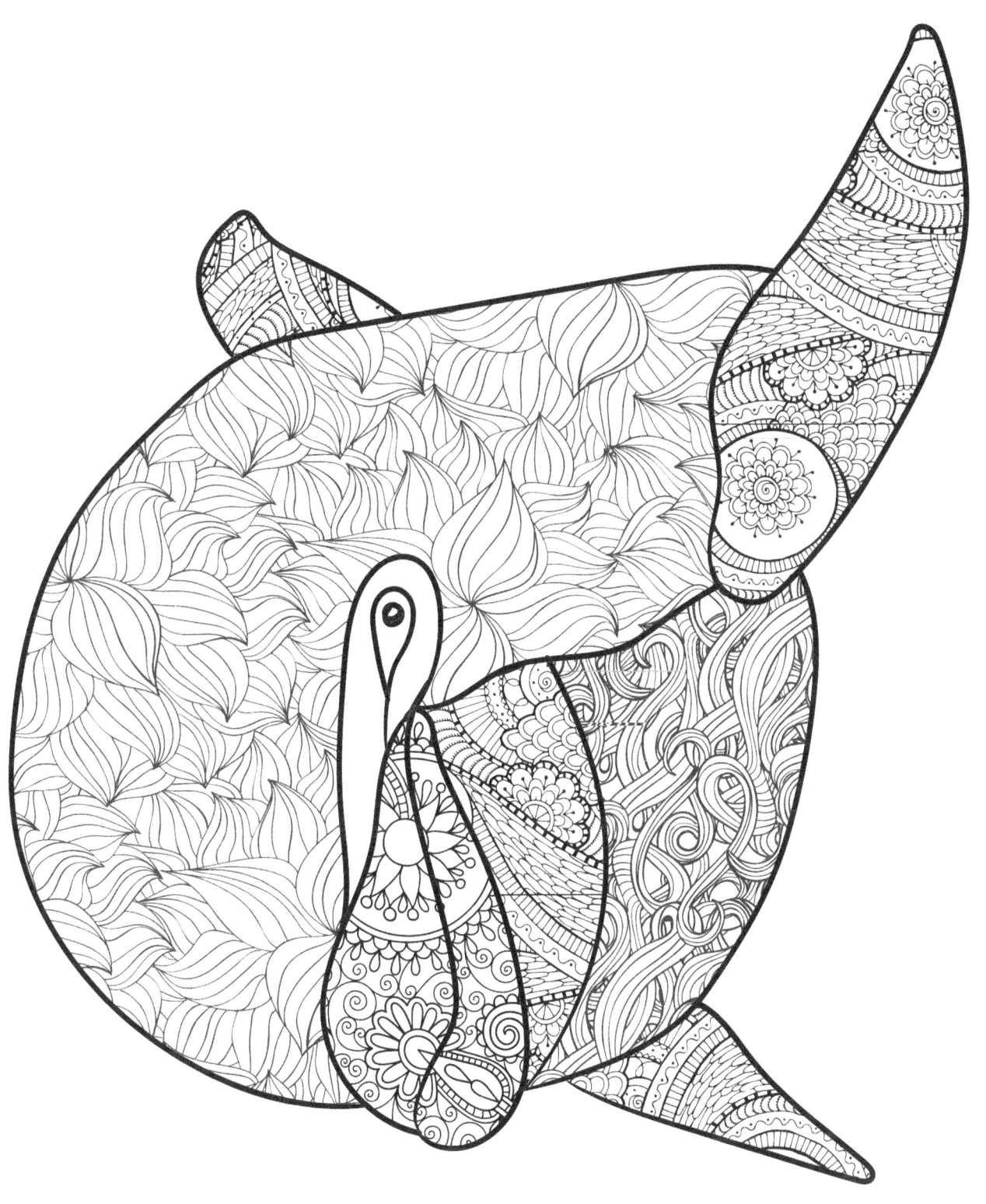

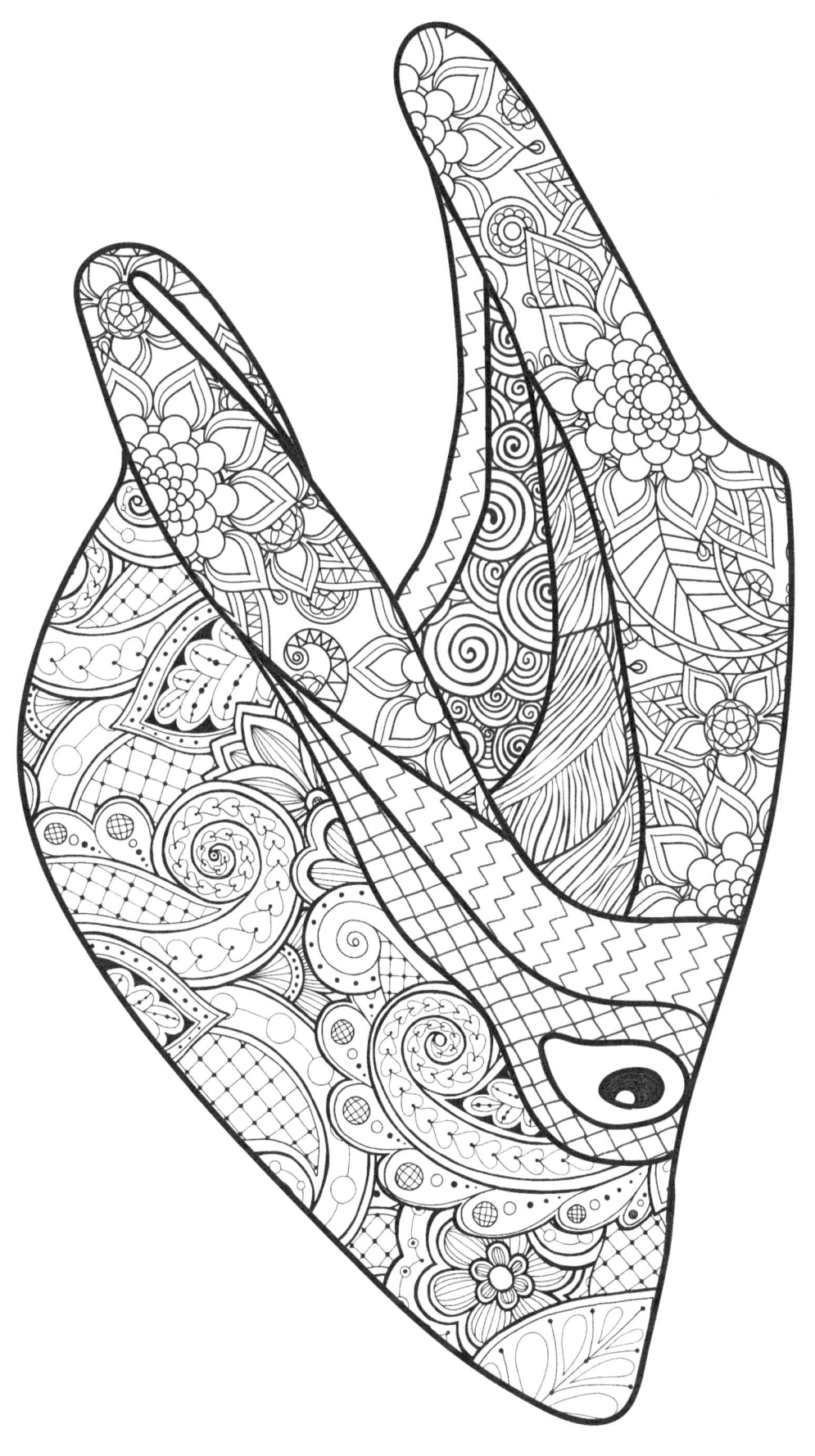

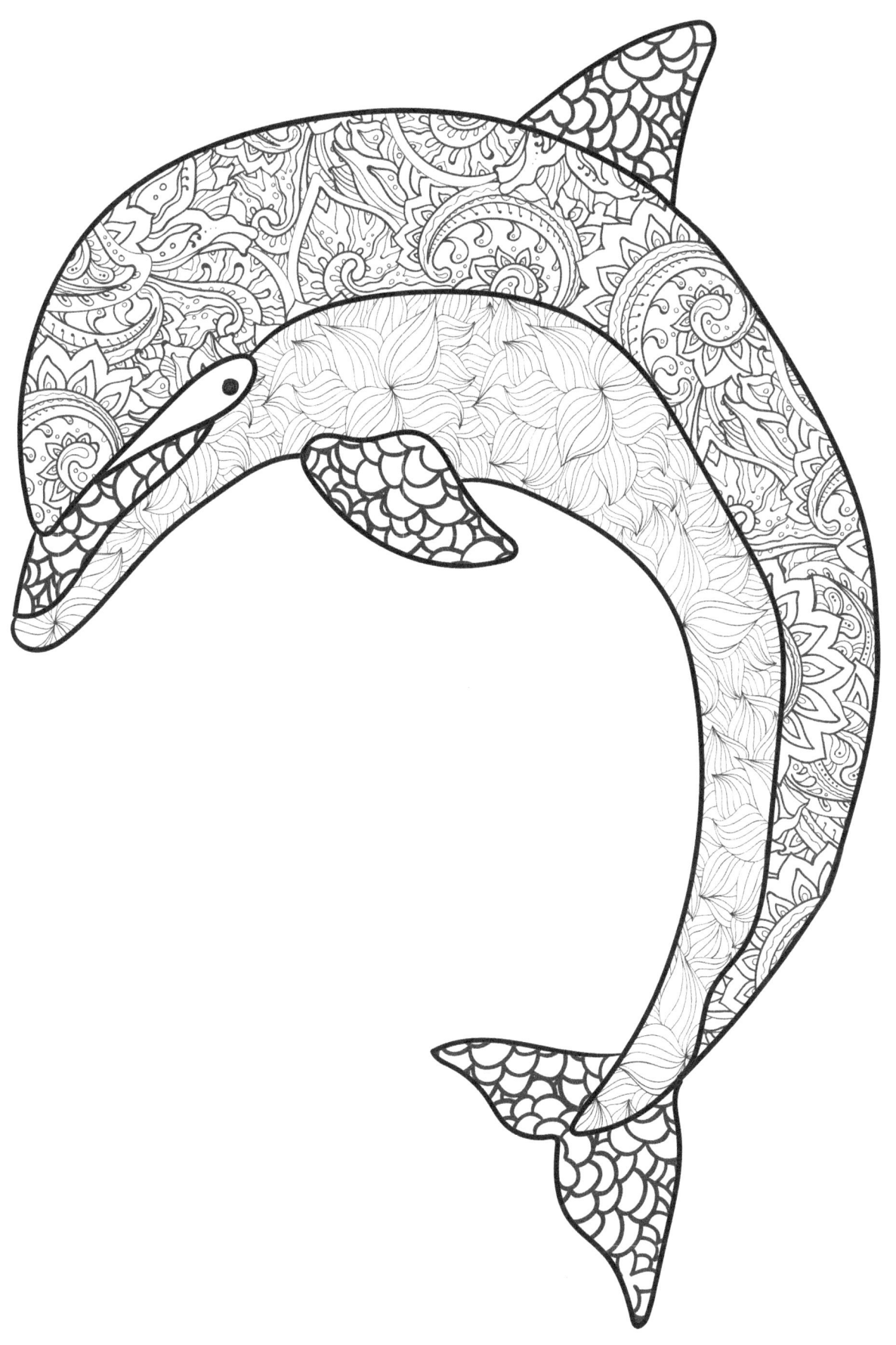

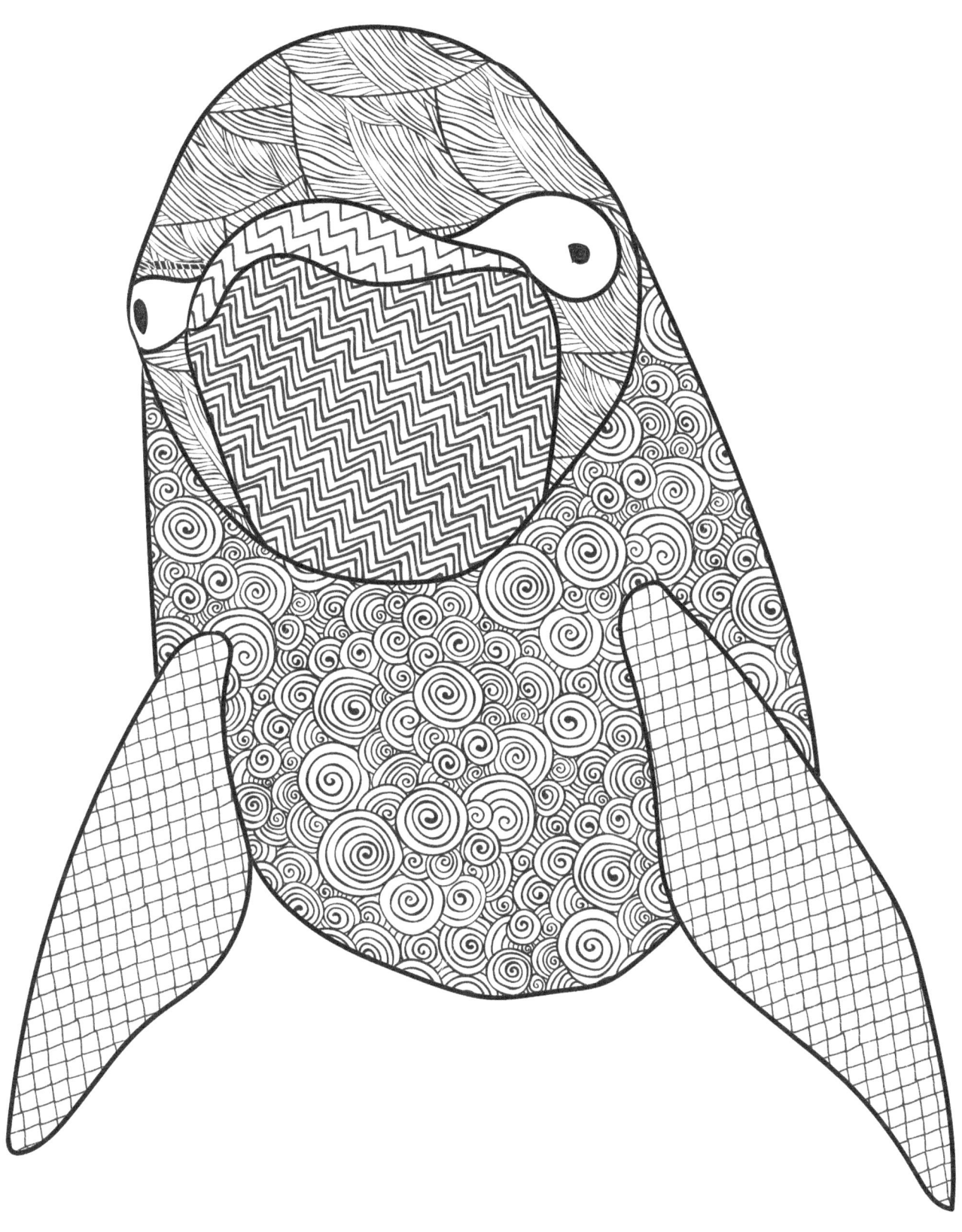

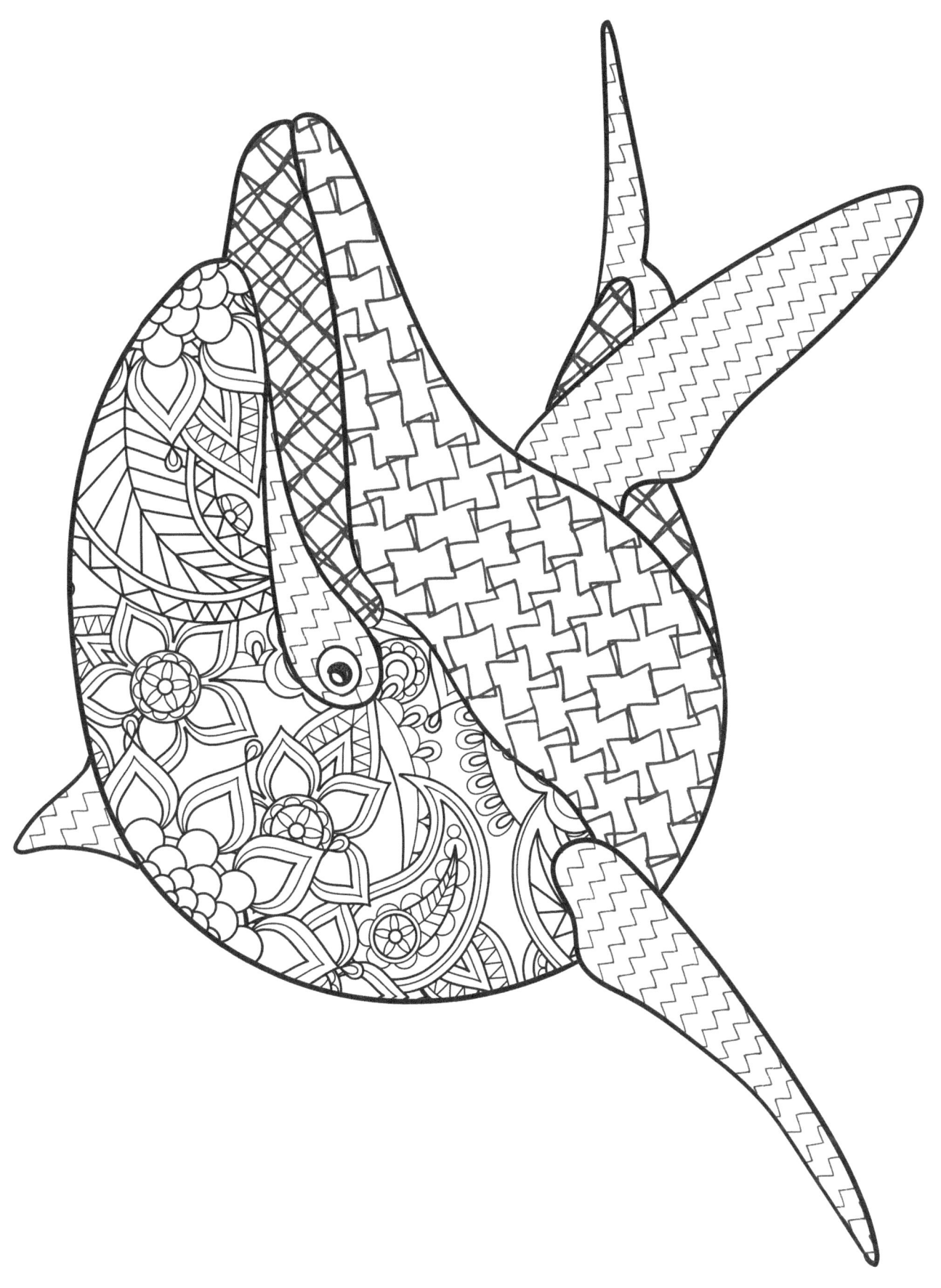

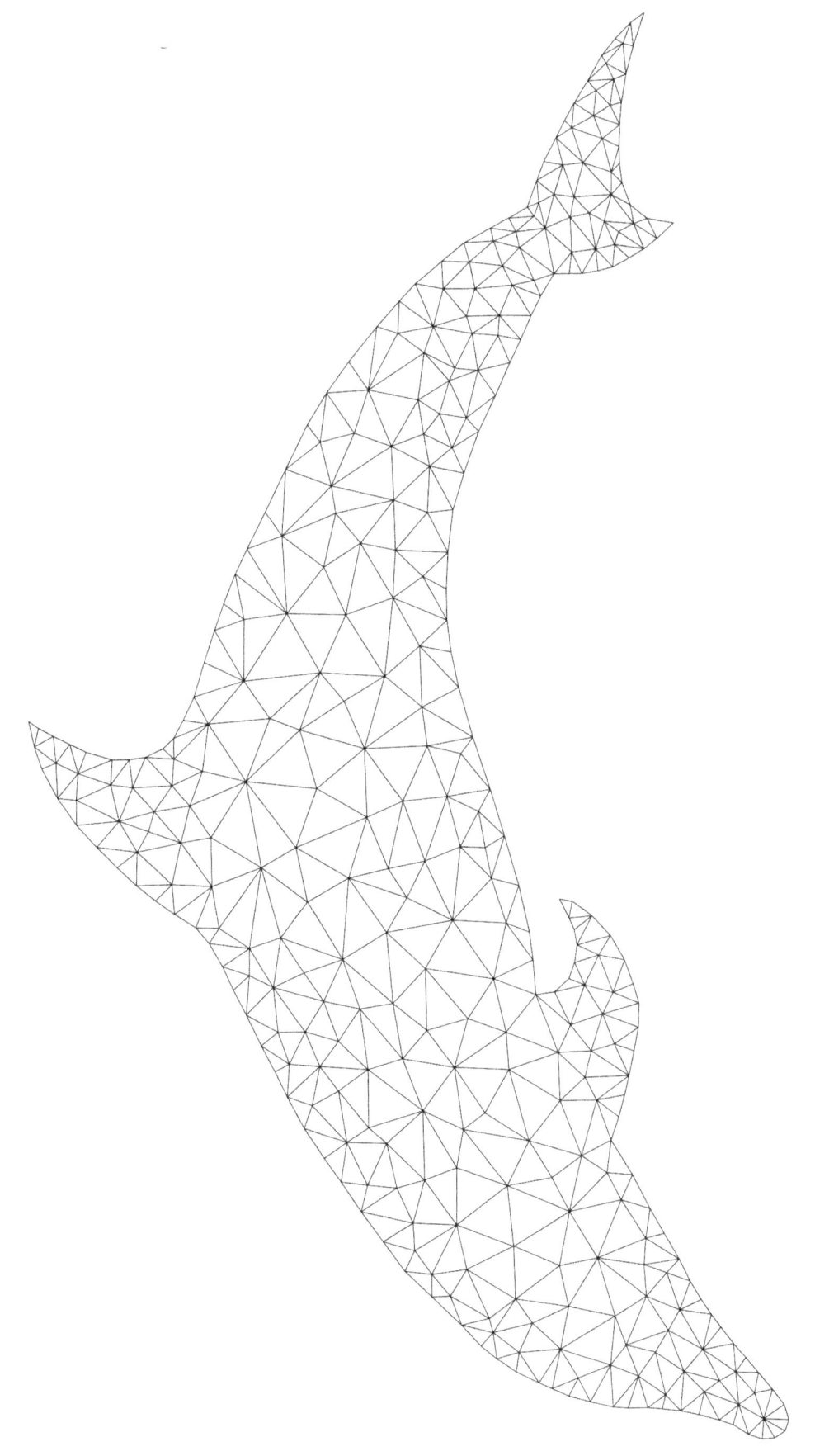

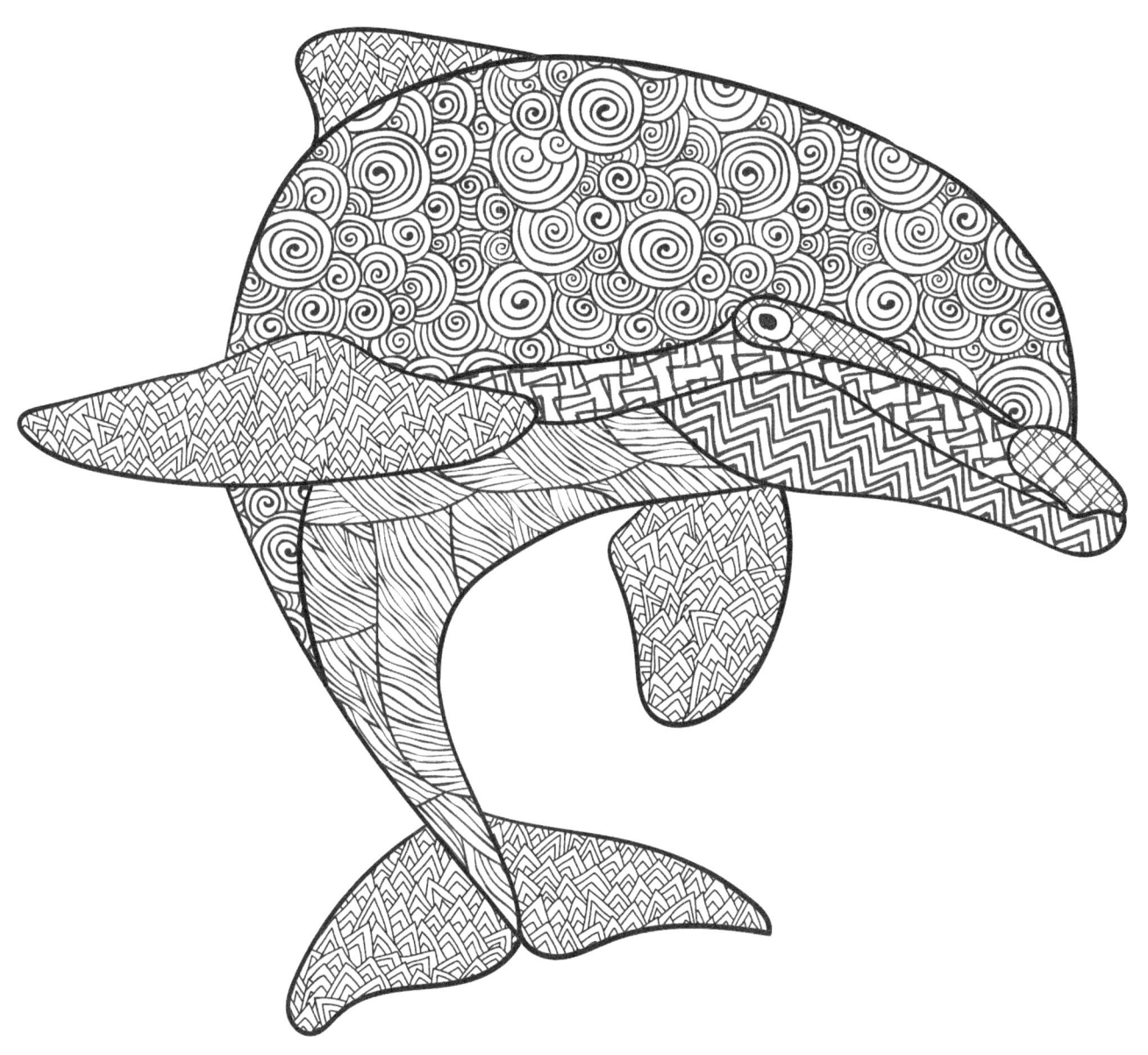

www.ingramcontent.com/pod-product-compliance
Lightning Source LLC
Chambersburg PA
CBHW081408280526
45788CB00009B/3029